Soccer Rules OK

Soccer Rules OK

Geoff Hales

Illustrations by Bryan Flaherty

A & C Black · London

To Jim Sharkey for the pleasure of seeing him play, and to Andy Reed for the pleasure of hearing him talk about it.

First published 1988 by
A & C Black (Publishers) Limited
35 Bedford Row, London WC1R 4JH

© 1988 Geoff Hales

ISBN 0 7136 5616 6

British Library Cataloguing in Publication Data

Hales, Geoff
  Soccer rules OK.
  1. Association football – Humour
  I. Title
  796.334'0207
  ISBN 0–7136–5616–6

Printed and bound in Great Britain by
Billing & Sons Limited, Worcester

Contents

Acknowledgement
The author and publisher are grateful for the advice and
assistance given by Reg Paine, former Referees' Secretary
at The Football Association.

Introduction

Soccer is the world's most popular game. Millions of
players are addicted to it, from the international superstar
who changes clubs at a signing-on fee that would make
J R Ewing blink to the ten-year-old hopeful who prays
every night that Sir will pick him for the Suez Road
Church of England Primary School team for the game
against All Saints' Under Twelves. Some spectators travel
hundreds of miles and endure extremes of cold and wet a
penguin wouldn't put up with to watch ninety minutes of
this compelling sport, and my mate Perce, who describes
himself as a goalkeeper, once said he'd rather save a
penalty than go out with Bo Derek. He's never managed
either, but it shows you how much the game means to some
of us.

It's such a simple game, too. All you need are two feet
and a ball. Standing on one foot, you kick the ball with the

other. If the ball goes into a net which is stretched between two posts and suspended from a crossbar, that's a goal. You have ten chaps to help you, and there are eleven other chaps trying to stop you. If after ninety minutes you've scored more goals than the other side, you've won. It could hardly be easier.

Because it's such an uncomplicated game, soccer doesn't require many rules, but it does need a few. There are, in fact, seventeen Laws, and it's surprising how many players and spectators don't know them. Perhaps this is because we just grow up kicking a ball about and never learn the rules properly, if at all. Even some of the people called on to run the line at minor league and cup games (often the substitute or the manager or someone's Dad who says he doesn't mind having a go till half-time) don't actually know what is or isn't off-side. Asked by the referee to watch the opposing forward line, some of these reluctant heroes rely on a sort of instinct, which usually lets them down, and it is not unknown for club linesmen and people's Dads to be prejudiced. This causes bad feeling and makes the referee's job even more difficult. Volunteer linesmen ought to know what they're doing, or they can be more trouble than they're worth.

Players need to know the Laws, too. At best, you will waste a lot of breath arguing with the referee when you haven't a leg to stand on, and at worst, if foul or abusive language is used, you could find that your conversation bores him and he's sent you off. Verbal dissent, even without foul or abusive language, can well result in the issue of a caution. This can be a nasty shock. As for spectators—well, you obviously can't be sent off because you're not on to start with, but you'll have a much better idea of what's going on if you have a look at the rules some time. Do you know, for instance, what happens if a throw-in goes directly into goal? Or what the rule is about encroaching into the area when a penalty's being taken? Read on, folks. This book tells you.

The playing area

The pitch

Most of us began playing soccer in the garden, on the
beach or in the school playground. Perce and I began in
the road outside our houses. We would take our jumpers
off, pile them up, measure eight paces between them and
then take it in turns to be Bobby Charlton and Gordon
Banks. The game went on till Perce's Mum came out and
told him to put his jumper on or he'd catch his death of
cold and have to miss school, or the tennis ball went into
someone's garden (with the score at 27–26) and neither of
us had the bottle to go and fetch it. It wasn't till much later
that we got onto a proper pitch, with lines and goalposts
and crossbars and similar luxuries, and had a real ball,
brown leather with laces.

There is no one permitted size for a pitch, but there are
maximum and minimum sizes, and the field should always
be rectangular, i.e. longer than it is wide. For international

matches, the pitch should be at most 120 yards (110 metres) and at least 110 yards (100 metres) long by at most 80 yards (75 metres) and at least 70 yards (64 metres) wide. In World Cup Final matches it is necessary for the pitch to be 115 yards × 75 yards, which in metric measurements is 105 metres × 69.5 metres. So, the next time you organise a World Cup Final, you'll know what to do. For those of us who don't quite make it to the national squad, the maximum length is 130 yards (120 metres) and the minimum is 100 yards (90 metres), while the maximum width is 100 yards (90 metres) and the minimum is 50 yards (45 metres).

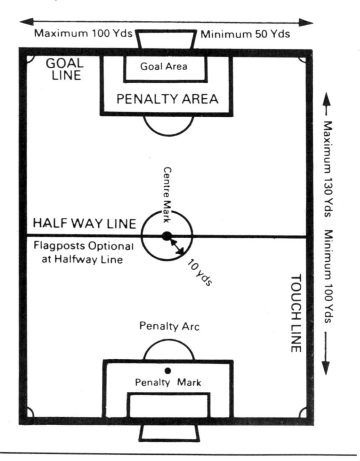

The field of play is marked by white lines which frequently have a thickness of between 2½" and 3" (64–76mm) in width. However, the law requires that the lines shall be 'not more than 5" (127mm) in width'. The length of the touch-lines and goal-lines is variable, as we have seen, but within these lines other dimensions are always the same. The centre circle has a 10-yard (9.15m) radius. The penalty area is 44 yards (40.32m) across by 18 yards (16.5m), and the penalty arc, which, by the way, is not part of the penalty area, is 10 yards (9.15m) from the penalty spot, which is 12 yards (11m) from the goal-line. The goal area is 20 yards (18.30m) by 6 yards (5.5m). This is why it is called the six-yard box. The arc at each corner of the field is 1 yard (1m for these purposes) from the corner flag, which must be at least 5 feet (1.5m) high. If there is a flag at the half-way line, it must be at least 1 yard back from the touch-line, and must also be at least 5 feet high. This minimum height is for the safety of the players, and for the same reason the flag-posts should not be pointed at the top or be too firmly fixed in the ground. Corner flag-posts, incidentally, must not be removed or pushed aside to make more room for the kicker when a corner-kick is being taken.

The goals

Everybody knows that the goal-posts are 8 feet (2.44m) high—that is, the underside of the cross-bar is 8 feet off the ground—and that the bar is 8 yards (7.32m) long, not counting the width of the posts. The cross-bar and posts can be made of wood or metal, and may be 'square, rectangular, round, half round, or elliptical in shape' as Law 1 puts it. The width and depth of the goal-posts and cross-bar must be no more than five inches (127mm), which is the same as the maximum thickness of goal-lines. Cross-bar, goal-posts and goal-lines must all be of the same thickness, so that they 'will conform in the same interior and exterior edges' (Law 1 again).

The posts and bar should be painted white, as most people who are likely to be reading this book will know already. What is less well known is what happens on those rare occasions when a cross-bar is broken in the course of a match. If this does occur, the game must be stopped and, unless the bar can be repaired or replaced satisfactorily, abandoned. However, in a friendly match, the teams can agree to use a rope, or to continue with nothing at all between the tops of the posts. In that situation, the referee has the unenviable job of deciding whether the ball went over or under where the cross-bar ought to have been.

Nets, which were introduced to stop arguments about which side of the posts the ball went, or whether it went over or under the bar—Perce and I used to have this problem in our jumper-and-tennis-ball days—are not actually compulsory, though most competitions do require you to use them. If you have nets, they need to be pegged down firmly and attached in such a way that they do not impede the goalkeeper or threaten to tangle anyone up. The referee is advised by the F.A. to check well in advance of the kick-off that they are properly pegged down and that the only holes are the ones that you'd expect a net to have. And if you were thinking of having a net made of wire mesh, don't. It's dangerous stuff, and anyway, you're playing soccer, not keeping chickens.

The goals can, by the way, be smaller in matches between teams 'of school age'.

Equipment

The ball

This important piece of equipment must, unsurprisingly, be spherical (look up Law 2 if you don't believe me). It must be made of leather 'or other approved materials' (as certified by the International Board). It has to have a circumference of 27 to 28 inches (0.68 to 0.71m) and must weigh between 14 and 16 ounces (396 and 453 grams) at the start of a game. With the water-proof coating which Science has provided for us, the ball is in fact likely to remain at a constant weight throughout the whole ninety minutes of a game, even on the muddiest afternoon.

Law 2 also specifies the pressure of the ball, which should be 'equal to 0.6–1.1 atmosphere (= 600–1,100 gr/cm^2)'. Those who like their measurements Imperial may prefer to know that this means 8.5–15.6 lb per square inch. These measurements are, of course, what is required at sea level, so bring your altimeter. Correct pressure is usually checked by giving the ball a good thump and seeing if it feels all right.

It is usually preferable to have a 'harder' ball on a soft pitch and a slightly 'softer' ball on a very hard pitch.

Boots and personal kit

As metal bars on the sole of the boot, and certain types of stud, can be dangerous in a tackle or challenge, there are regulations about what you can wear on your feet. Reputable boot manufacturers, of course, conform to these regulations. However, referees and linesmen may have a duty to check the safety of the boots when a substitute is about to come on, depending on the rules of the competition, and can have a look at anyone's boots at any time. This is in accordance with Law 4, which begins by saying that a player 'shall not wear anything which is dangerous to another player' and goes into great detail on the subject of boots.

There are two sorts of studs in common use: the moulded and the independently replaceable. The moulded ones are usually made of rubber, plastic or polyurethene. The minimum diameter for these is $\frac{3}{8}''$ (10mm) where there are at least ten studs on the boot; anything smaller than that across the top might be too pointed to be safe in a tackle. The independently attached studs, which must be solid, can be made of leather, soft rubber, plastic or aluminium. They must be 'round in plan' and cylindrical or cone-shaped, and must be at least $\frac{1}{2}''$ (13mm) in diameter at the narrowest point. No stud, of either kind, may project more than $\frac{3}{4}''$ (20mm) from the sole of the boot.

If bars are worn, or a combination of bars and studs, the bars must go across the full width of the sole, be at least $\frac{1}{2}''$ wide and be rounded at the corners. Like studs, they must not stick out more than $\frac{3}{4}''$. Metal plates are not allowed

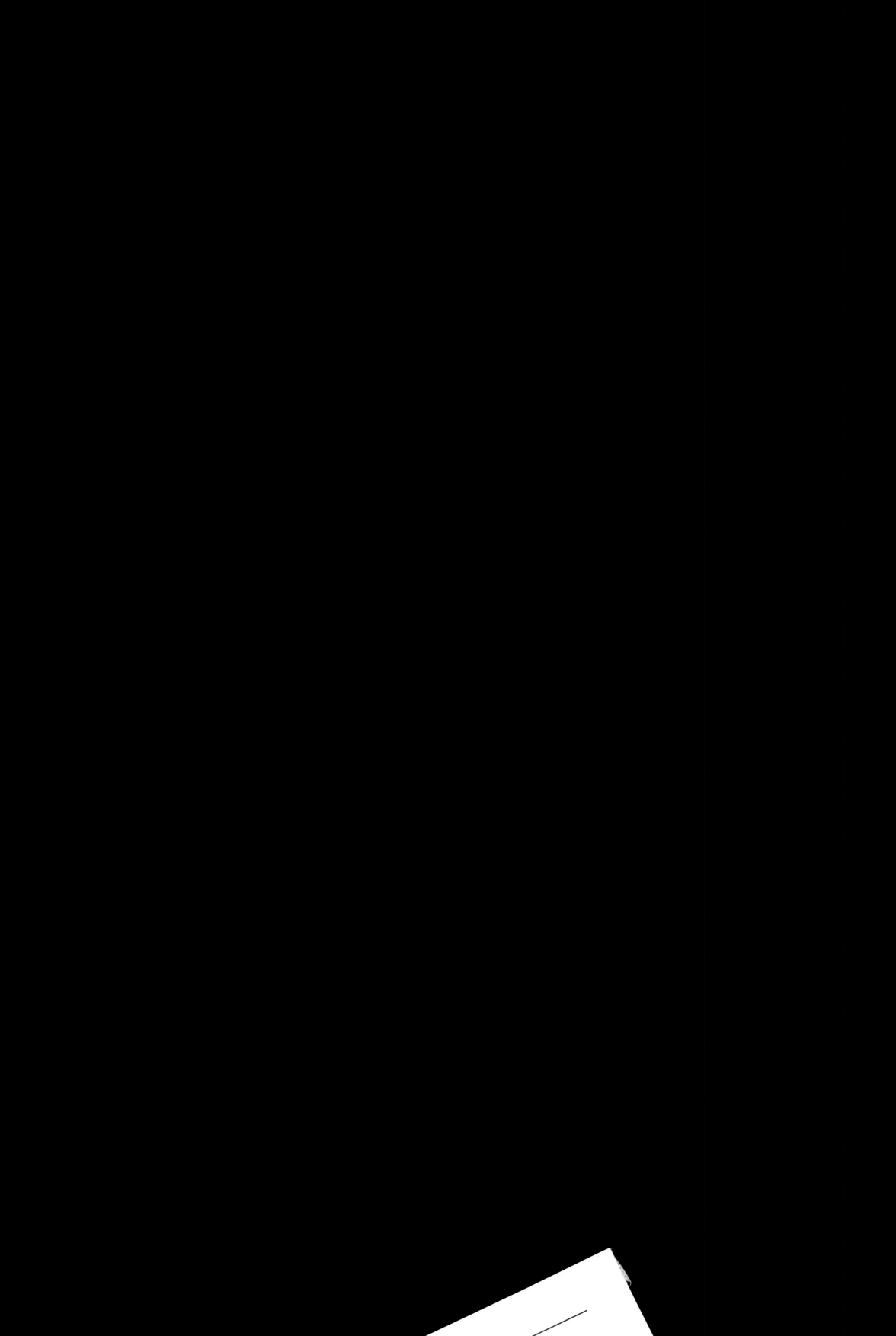

Teams and times

Soccer is usually played between two teams of eleven players. Law 3 actually says 'not more than eleven, one of whom shall be the goalkeeper', but goes on to say that the International Board 'is of the opinion that a match should not be considered valid if there are fewer than seven players in either of the teams'. This does not invalidate five- and six-a-side matches, of course, which have their own rules and regulations.

In addition to the eleven, teams may also have one or more substitutes, but the number, if permitted, depends entirely on the rules of the individual competition. In friendlies as many as five can be used, as long as the number is agreed before the kick-off and someone tells the referee, who likes to know this sort of thing. How and when substitutions can be made is explained on page 30.

A game normally lasts ninety minutes, and is divided into two halves of forty-five minutes each. However, certain competitions may permit a reduction in the length of the game, and in women's football and in junior matches a shorter time can be played. In many knock-out ('Cup') competitions, games that are level after ninety minutes can be extended by playing two fifteen-minute periods of 'extra time', with perhaps a penalty shoot-out to follow that if the scores are still level. (Regulations for penalty shoot-outs are to be found on pages 37 and 38 of 'Referees' Chart and Players' Guide to the Laws of Association Football, 1987–1988', authorised by the International Football Association Board.)

The referee is expected to add on whatever injury time he thinks necessary—that is, playing time lost through injury or for some other reason, for example the need to replace a lost or burst ball. This is added on at the end of the half in which it occurs, not at the end of the ninety minutes. The referee must also extend time at the end of either half for the taking of a penalty when the offence occurs in normal time but when the final whistle would have been due before the kick could be taken.

According to Law 7, the half-time interval is five minutes in professional football, although the referee may agree to the interval being extended (but he is advised, in Law 8, to

do this only 'in very exceptional circumstances'). There are times, too, when an interval could be dispensed with altogether, for instance when the weather is particularly foul and there is nowhere to go to get out of it. It could also happen on a winter afternoon when it is obviously going to get too dark for play if time is lost for the team-talk and the oranges. As many minor matches take place on grounds where there are no dressing-rooms and no floodlights, it makes sense for the referee to say, 'Turn straight round, lads' and to re-start play at once. It should be pointed out, however, that players have a right to an interval, irrespective of the referee's decision.

The Law does not specify how much time is allowed between the end of normal time and the start of extra time. This is left to the referee.

The game

The kick-off

On winning the toss, it is usual for the successful captain to choose which end to attack, but he can simply opt to take the kick-off (or 'place-kick' as it is officially called in Law 8). The second half is started by the other team, without a further spin of the coin, but if extra time is necessary, you do have to toss again.

At the kick-off, all members of the team not taking the kick must be at least ten yards (9.15 m) from the centre-spot, which is what the centre-circle is there for. They must remain outside the circle until the ball has been kicked off. The ball is not considered to be in play until it has travelled the 27"–28" of its own circumference. In addition, all players must be in their own half of the field.

The ball must go forward, into the opposition's half, and the kicker must not touch the ball again until it has been touched or played by someone else; if he does, the opposition is awarded an indirect free kick. If an opposing player moves into the centre circle or any player moves into enemy territory before the ball is in play, the kick is taken again. The same applies if the ball is not played forward.

You can't score a goal direct from the kick-off. It seems a shame to discourage sides who like to attack from the start, but there it is.

Out of play

The ball is out of play when it has completely crossed the touch-line or the goal-line, in the air or on the ground. That is to say, as long as any part of the ball is on the line or above it, it is still in play. It is worth knowing that it is the *outside* edge of the line which marks the boundary of the playing area. The ball is also 'out of play' when the game is stopped by the referee, even though the ball may actually be in the playing area.

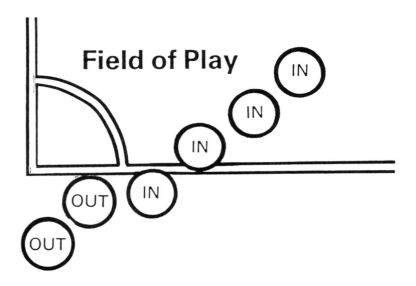

The ball is out of play when it completely crosses a line in the air but then swerves or is blown back in again, for instance at a corner. Once it has crossed a line it is out of play, regardless of where it finishes up. It is also out of play if it is completely over a line but is being held by the goalkeeper inside his area—it is the position of the ball that counts. Similarly, the ball is in play even if the player playing it is entirely outside the playing area, but the ball itself is on or above the line. The ball is also still in play if it rebounds from the corner-flag post or the woodwork, and if it hits one of the officials when he is within the playing area. And if the ball goes into goal off the referee or a linesman, that counts. 'Advice to Referees' following Law 9 says that linesmen 'should, as far as possible, keep out of the field of play' to prevent that sort of thing occurring. The referee simply has to do his best to keep out of the way of the ball, but if it hits him, the teams have to carry on, whatever happens.

If the ball goes out of play over the goal-line, the referee will award a goal, a goal-kick or a corner; if it goes out over the touch-line, a throw-in will follow.

Throw-ins

Throw-ins are taken at the point where the ball crossed the line, as indicated by the linesman. This means on or near the line itself, not ten yards back from it, and not five or ten yards further along it. Players who try to gain a few extra yards by shuffling along or taking a run-up along the line should not look terribly hurt or have a tantrum if told to take the ball back to where it crossed the line, since what they are doing is called, in plain language, cheating. It's now deemed a foul throw if you succumb to this sort of low behaviour.

When taking a throw, the thrower must be facing the field of play. Don't stand with your back to it with the ball in front of your face and throw the ball back over your head. No one loves a smart-ass. Law 15 states that the ball must be thrown from behind and over the head, and you must really throw it, not just drop it. You must use both hands to throw the ball; it's not enough to hold the ball in one hand and have the other one just touching it. That is one of the infringements for which a foul throw may be awarded.

The thrower must also have a part of each foot on or behind the touch-line at the moment the ball is thrown. If you lift your feet as you throw so that you are on your toes in front of the line and no part of your foot is behind or touching it, that's a foul throw, even if your heels are above the line or behind it. The punishment for a foul throw is that the throw goes to the opposition.

The ball is considered to be in play as soon as it crosses the line, and anyone can then attempt to play it. That is, of course, except for the thrower, who is not allowed to play it a second time until someone else has touched or played it; if he does, that's an indirect free kick to the opposition, to be taken at the scene of the crime.

Two final points here. Although you may be in an off-side position, you cannot be penalised if you receive the ball direct from a throw-in—but once a player other than the thrower has the ball, you might be. And, although a goalkeeper can score a goal with a clearance throw, you can't score direct from a throw-in.

But what happens if you do? Well, if you throw the ball directly into your opponent's goal, a goal kick will be awarded, and if you manage to throw it straight into your own, it's a corner, though the opposition will be yelling their heads off for a goal.

Goal kicks

A goal kick is given if the ball is put over the goal-line, but not of course into the net, by an attacker. The kick can be taken by any member of the defending side, from any point within the six-yard box on that side of the goal where the ball crossed the line. In other words, if the ball went out of play between the left goal-post and the left corner-flag, the kick is taken from the left side of the goal area. It does not have to be taken from the corner of the six-yard box, though it often is.

The ball must pass outside the penalty area directly from the kick and attackers must stay outside the area until it has done so. Other defenders can be in the area, however. This means that a defender other than the 'keeper can take the kick, while the 'keeper stays on his line. We have all known weak goal kicks taken by the 'keeper that are kicked or headed straight back into the net by lurking forwards, leaving the defenders to say 'Bad luck, Terry!' without really meaning it.

If the kick is intercepted inside the penalty area, by defender or attacker, it must be taken again. Once the ball is outside the area, it must be touched by another player before the kicker can play it again. As usual, it's an indirect free-kick if you play it twice. So, if you miskick straight to the opposing number nine, you have to recover the ball somehow before it leaves the area. That's all right, because it's not in play till it does so. All that would happen here is that the kick would have to be re-taken.

Law 16, the one that deals with goal kicks, also says that a goalkeeper 'shall not receive the ball into his hands from a goal-kick in order that he may thereafter kick it into play'. You can, of course, play it to him as long as he lets it go out of the area and then plays it back in again before picking it up and punting it downfield. He could score by doing that, but you are not allowed to blast a goal kick direct into your opponent's net.

By the way, you can't be penalised for being in an off-side position if you receive the ball direct from a goal kick. The same applies to corners, which we look at now.

Corners

If a defender puts the ball over the goal-line but not into the goal, the result is, of course, a corner. You probably knew that if you've played a bit!

A corner kick is taken from the quarter-circle marked inside each corner of the field—to be exact, from the corner nearest the point at which the ball went out of play. The ball must be placed wholly within the quarter-circle; no part of it must be outside the furthest edge of the goal-line, touch-line or curved line. In other words, the thickness of the line is part of the quarter-circle. You are not allowed to move the corner-flag or bend it back to give yourself a better run at the ball.

Defenders must stand at least ten yards from the ball until it is in play, which, as usual, means when it has gone the distance of its own circumference. Another attacker or attackers may stand nearer. The taker of the kick must not play the ball a second time until another player has touched it, even if it comes back to him directly off the goal-post, which can happen. For committing this headstrong act, the kicker gives away an indirect free kick.

A goal can be scored directly from a corner, and another bonus for attackers is that, as I said earlier, it is technically impossible to be off-side when receiving the ball from a corner, since you could not possibly be in front of the ball when it was played. But as soon as someone behind you plays the ball, you could be pulled up, since you would then be between the ball and the goal. See the section on 'off-side', where all the grisly possibilities are thoroughly explored. This treat is to be found on pages 32–7.

Dropped ball

When play has been interrupted for some reason, such as an injury to a player (not caused by a foul) or to an official, the game is re-started by the referee dropping the ball. This could also occur when there has been crowd interference, if the ball bursts or if two players have the ball stuck somewhere between them and seem unlikely to be able to get it out without causing each other a bit of damage. Law 8 sums it up by saying the ball is dropped 'after a temporary suspension of play from any cause not mentioned elsewhere in these Laws'. If, of course, the stoppage is caused by a foul or other infringement, the re-start is usually by a free kick.

The ball is dropped where it was when play was suspended, unless the incident took place in the goal area, in which case the ball is dropped on the nearest point of the goal area line, parallel to the goal-line. It is in play only when it reaches the ground, and if either of the two players between whom it is dropped cannot wait that long and takes a swing at it before it lands, the ball has to be dropped again. Perhaps this is a good point to remind those players taking part in this quaint little ceremony that the ball is the target, not the other bloke's shins, however much you dislike his political opinions or his poncey aftershave.

Bringing on the sub

Players can be substituted for any reason and at any time. A maximum of two substitutes is permitted in competitive matches, depending on the rules of the competition, but up to five may be used in friendly matches, providing the requirements of the law are adhered to. There are strict regulations, set out in Law 3, about how the substitution must be made. You can bring on a sub only if play has already been stopped. The ref has to be told beforehand that the substitution is going to be made and the sub cannot come on until the player he is replacing has gone off. The referee must signal him on, and he must enter at the half-way line. If it is the requirement of the competition, he must also have his studs checked (see 'Boots and personal kit'). The player going off is not allowed to take any further part in the game.

If the sub comes on without the referee's permission, he is liable to be cautioned; that is, 'to be booked'. The game is then re-started with a dropped ball. Players can enter, re-enter or leave the field during play only with the referee's blessing. So, no popping off for a quick lie-down and popping back on again when you feel like it.

In the 'Advice to referees' section that follows Law 3, the F.A. warns that a player 'who leaves the field for any reason must not take part in another match until that in which he commenced is ended'. Somebody must have heard the story of a park team who took off their ace striker after he'd scored a hat-trick and immediately sent him on as sub for their reserves who were playing an important cup match two pitches away. He broke his ankle and was out for the rest of the season.

Subs still on the bench, like everyone else, are subject to the Laws and you can actually be cautioned or even sent off while still in the dug-out for such offences as using 'foul or abusive language' or showing dissent. The same applies to club officials, who have been known to get over-excited. Curiously, a 'named substitute' is allowed for a player who is sent off before the match starts, perhaps for some atrocity committed in the tunnel or during the kick-about, but of course you cannot bring on a sub for somebody dismissed once play has begun.

Changing goalkeepers during the game is permitted, provided that you tell the referee before you make the change and that the change is made during a stoppage. Referees are advised that they should 'until informed of a change, allow no other player to take up or claim the privileges attached to the position'.

Off-side

Of all the laws of soccer, off-side is the one that causes the most trouble. A linesman has only to signal and all the old jokes about guide dogs and white sticks come out ('Haven't you read the rules, ref?', 'He can't, they don't do 'em in Braille!'). Referees with 20/20 vision are given the addresses of competent opticians, and linesmen are showered with well-meaning advice about what to do with their flags.

The controversy is not because off-side is really such a difficult idea to take in. The problem is that referee and linesmen have to make snap decisions about a series of events that occur very quickly. Not only do they have to decide what happened—they must also make a judgement about whether an attacker is interfering with play or with an opponent, or seeking to gain an advantage. The officials can take comfort from the thought that at least half the spectators are in a better position to see and have a more highly developed sense of right and wrong than they have. Even if they get it right, all they can expect from a grateful public is an ironic 'Saw that one, didn't you?'

The Law itself (Law 11) is fairly simple. You will be off-side if you are nearer to the opponents' goal-line than the ball and there are fewer than two opposing players (possibly, but not necessarily, including the goalkeeper) between yourself and the opposition's goal-line when the ball is played by one of your own side. The referee must also be satisfied that you are interfering with play, if only by taking the attention of an opponent, or that you are attempting to gain some advantage from being where you are. So, it is possible to be in an off-side position without being penalised. It is, of course, up to the referee to decide whether or not you are interfering with play.

There are two points to note here. The first is that you can be parallel with the ball when it is played and can still be on-side, since the law says you must be nearer to the opposition's goal-line than the ball is. The second point is that at least two opponents must be *nearer* the goal-line than you are to put you on-side—one standing the same distance from the goal-line does not count.

You cannot be off-side if you are in your own half at the
moment the ball is played, and you cannot be off-side if you
receive the ball direct from a goal kick, a corner or a
throw-in. And you can't be off-side when the ball has been
dropped by the referee.

Law 11 says that you are penalised for off-side if you are
in an off-side position and are interfering with play (or an
opponent, or seeking to gain an advantage) when the ball
is played by or touches a member of your own team. There
is a possible problem here. What happens if you're in an
off-side position when a ball played to you by one of your
own team-mates hits one of the opposition in flight and
then comes to you? Are you off-side or not? It could be
argued that you actually received the ball from an
opponent. Well, the answer is that you *are* off-side; you
were off-side at the moment the ball was played by one of
your own team, and it should be signalled as soon as it
happens. What the ball did after that has nothing to do
with it. (It would be different, of course, if the other team
was in possession and made you a present of the ball.)

To repeat: it is where you were when one of your own team played the ball that is important. It doesn't matter where you were when you received it, or whether it hit an opponent, the referee or the woodwork on the way. For the same reason, you cannot put yourself on-side by running back if you were off-side when the ball was played.

For off-side, an indirect free kick is awarded, which is taken from where the offence occurred. However, if you were caught off-side in the six-yard box, the kick could be taken from anywhere on that side of the area. This is to avoid a situation where the kick might have to be taken from an awkward position, for instance, right in front of a goal-post where the kicker could not get a good run at it. This, by the way, applies to all free kicks for the defending team inside the goal area.

Off-side is one of the offences for which an indirect free kick is awarded. Others include:

● dissent and certain forms of ungentlemanly conduct (see 'Cautions', pages 60–1)
● dangerous play
● obstruction
● charging fairly when the ball is not within the playing distance
● charging the goalkeeper unfairly, as explained below
● time-wasting by the goalkeeper, when the ball is in play
● as a goalkeeper, taking more than four steps with the ball.

In each case, the referee must decide whether the offence is deliberate. Accidental infringements are not penalised.

Dangerous play

Dangerous play is not the same thing as an attempt to injure an opponent, which could easily be a sending-off offence. It is, however, 'a fair intentional act committed without due regard to the safety of one's opponent'. It might occur, for instance, when in order to make contact with the ball, a player raises his boot so high that he might kick in the face a member of the other team who is trying to head it. Attempting to kick the ball while it is in the goalkeeper's hands is another example of what Law 12 calls playing 'in a manner considered by the Referee to be dangerous'—in fact, this is the one the law cites. You may not be trying to break the goalkeeper's fingers, but you could still do it.

Obstruction

This is a deliberate attempt to prevent an opponent from getting to the ball when you are not playing it yourself and it is not within playing distance. Running between an opponent and the ball to prevent him from reaching it is not allowed, and neither is 'interposing the body to form an

obstacle to an opponent' as Law 12 puts it. In other words, if you can't get the ball yourself, you must not simply set out to stop an opponent doing so. It's an indirect free kick if you do, though the referee may 'play the advantage' if the opponent reaches the ball and is able to play it anyway. You can, by the way, be fairly charged from behind (this does not mean charging in the back) if you are obstructing.

Obstruction is not the same as holding or pushing, which are direct free kick or penalty offences, and it is not the same as shielding the ball when the ball is within playing distance, when dribbling or when waiting for reinforcements to arrive. In those circumstances, the ball is in your possession and you are perfectly entitled to try to keep it by screening it. It is also perfectly fair to screen the ball while it runs out of play, so long as it is in playing distance.

Shoulder charging

In the last section, it was mentioned that you can charge an opponent from behind if he is obstructing you; and a player who deliberately turns his back when he is about to be tackled, may also be charged 'but not in a dangerous manner'. In all circumstances, a fair charge is 'with the shoulder', and neither player must push with his arms. The charge must not be violent or dangerous, and there is no licence for 'elbow to rib-cage' or 'arm across wind-pipe'. It's a game of football, not a martial arts demonstration, and the referee will award a direct free kick against anyone who thinks otherwise.

For a charge to be fair, the ball must also be within playing distance and the referee must be satisfied that both players are attempting to play it. If a charge is delivered 'fairly', that is, with the shoulder and with the arms and elbows tucked in, but 'off the ball', an indirect free kick is given.

To sum up—you can charge unfairly at the 'right' time, which is penalised by a direct free kick, or fairly at the 'wrong' time, for which the free kick is indirect.

There is often confusion about whether charging the goalkeeper is legal. (About my earliest footballing memory is of Perce and me weeping buckets when Peter McParland of Aston Villa charged Ray Wood of Manchester United over the line in the 1957 Cup Final and United lost. Perce actually set off down the road to 'do' him.) Law 12 provides that if the goalkeeper is in his goal area, he is entitled to a certain amount of protection. That is, you can charge the goalkeeper inside the six-yard box only if he is holding the ball or is deliberately obstructing. If he hasn't got the ball, and isn't obstructing, you can't. Once he is outside the goal area, you can charge him 'with the shoulder' whether he is holding the ball or not, as long as it is within playing distance and you are both attempting to play it.

The four-step rule

It is well known that the goalkeeper must not take more than four steps while holding the ball, which seems simple enough. But Law 12 ('Fouls And Misconduct') is careful to say exactly what is meant by this. The 'four steps' begin from the moment the 'keeper brings the ball under control with his hands. From then on, he must not take 'more than 4 steps in any direction whilst holding, bouncing or throwing the ball in the air and catching it again, without releasing it into play'. Once he has let it go into play, he must not touch it again with his hands until it has been touched or played by one of his own team outside the penalty area or by a member of the other team inside or outside the area. It does not matter whether the 'keeper released the ball on the first or the fourth step—he cannot, for instance, release it on the second step and have two 'in reserve'.

Once it is released, someone else has to touch it, in accordance with the provisos quoted in law where it is stated that the ball must have 'been touched or played by another player of the same team outside the penalty area, or by a player of the opposing team either inside or outside the penalty area' before the 'keeper can pick it up again.

The point of all this is to prevent the ball being played back and forth between the goalkeeper and the defenders inside the area to waste a few seconds, and to prevent the 'keeper from wasting time by hanging on to the ball for longer than necessary. The opposition gets an indirect free kick for this.

Free kicks

As everyone knows, there are two sorts of free kick, direct and indirect. You can score direct from a direct free kick (though not against your own team), but you can't from an indirect one. An indirect free kick is signalled by the referee raising one arm above his head. For a goal to be scored from an indirect free kick the ball must touch or be played by another player before it goes into the goal. No problem about that.

Free kicks are taken from the point where the offence for which they were given took place. There are two exceptions to this, however. First, if the kick is awarded to the defending team for an offence committed inside its own goal area, it can be taken from any point of that side of the goal area. Second, if an indirect free kick offence is committed by the defenders inside their own goal area, the attacking side takes the kick from the point on the part of the goal area line that runs parallel to the goal-line, nearest to where the incident happened. If an offence by the defending team within the goal area merited a direct free kick, the result would be a penalty and the question would not arise.

When a free kick is being taken, all members of the other team must remain at least ten yards away from the ball until it is in play, which means that it must have travelled the 27–28″ of its own circumference. This is fair enough, but what happens if the kick is being taken by the attacking side less than ten yards from the defenders' goal-line? Where can the defenders stand? It would be ridiculous if they were obliged to be ten yards behind or to the side of the ball, or behind the goal-line. In this situation, Law 13, the one that covers free kicks, allows defenders to stand on the goal-line between the goal-posts, though not anywhere else on the goal-line.

When a free kick is being taken by players inside their own penalty area the attackers must, of course, be ten yards away as usual, but they must also remain outside the penalty area till the ball is in play and has gone outside the area. If an attacker rushes into the area before the ball has left it, or comes within ten yards, the kick is delayed until, as the Law says, 'the Law is complied with'. The kick has to be re-taken if the ball does not go directly into play; this includes the possibility of a miskick sending the ball back over the goal-line, perhaps even into goal, which is unlikely but is not impossible.

Defenders are forbidden, by the way, to give the ball direct into the 'keeper's hands when taking a free kick inside their own penalty area 'in order that he may thereafter kick it into play'. The ball must leave the penalty area. If the kick is being taken outside the area, there is no reason why it should not be played straight to the 'keeper's hands so that he can boot it upfield.

As with a place kick, the kicker must not play the ball a second time before another player has touched it. If he does, that's an indirect free kick to the opposition from the point at which the second touch took place.

Failing to remove yourself the necessary ten yards from an opposition free kick is very bookable indeed; in fact, you can be sent off for doing it more than once. Players who don't comply can expect no mercy. (It's remarkable that the ones who are the slowest to retreat are the ones who yell the loudest when the opposition are slow to remove themselves.) The referee can use his discretion and allow a kick to be taken quickly, with opponents still in range, but you're still expected to get back. Kicking the ball away at a free kick is ungentlemanly conduct and is punished with a caution. And if you've already been booked, you can be sent off.

To end this section here is a quiz question. What happens if the ball goes direct into the other team's goal from an indirect free kick? Answer—it's a goal kick. One point if you knew that. For your bonus point, what happens if a player taking either a direct or an indirect free kick from outside his own penalty area puts the ball into his own net without it touching another player? That's a corner. And there is one more bizarre possibility. Suppose you take a free kick inside your own penalty area and kick it into play—outside the penalty area, that is— and the wind blows it back into the net? That's a corner, too.

Direct free kick offences

For the more serious offences against the Laws, a direct free kick is awarded. The offences meriting this are:

- charging violently or dangerously (see page 39)
- charging from behind, unless obstructed (see page 38)
- holding
- pushing
- striking or attempting to strike or spitting at an opponent
- kicking, or trying to kick, an opponent
- tripping an opponent
- jumping at an opponent
- handball.

The law (Law 12) makes it quite clear that these offences must be intentional. Accidental handball, for instance, does not result in a direct free kick even though the player handling might gain some advantage.

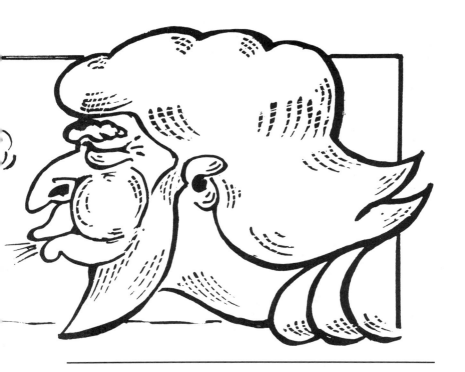

Holding and pushing

Obviously there are times in any physical sport where you lose your balance or need to protect yourself when, for instance, someone crashes into you. When that happens, you clearly need to use your hands and arms. This does not mean, however, that you are allowed to use them to pull an opponent back, perhaps by his shirt (which counts as holding), or to push him off the ball. You are not allowed to push with your hands even if you are being deliberately obstructed, though in such a situation you are allowed to charge from behind (see pages 38–9). Goalkeepers are not permitted to use the ball to push an opponent away.

The referee must, as always, be satisfied that the pushing or holding is intentional, and he will be looking out for deliberate infringements that can be made to look accidental. If you are standing two yards away from the ref holding a handful of shirt, it's not much good looking innocent or saying you didn't mean it. Spectators and players are alike in assuming referees to be corrupt, short-sighted and stupid, but they have their lucid moments.

Striking an opponent

It is hardly necessary to say that 'sticking one on' a member of the other side, however great the provocation, is very likely to get you sent off and probably suspended; and the same applies if you choose one of the officials to try your Frank Bruno routine on. Even if your swing doesn't land, the punishment is the same—trying to hit someone is enough. It is not only fists that count as offensive weapons. Deliberately throwing the ball 'vigorously' at an opponent is considered to be the same as striking him.

Spitting at an opponent or an official comes under the same heading. A bloke who used to play for us was sent off for spitting and claimed till the end of his career that he was only getting rid of his chewing gum and that it was sheer bad luck it landed on the referee's boot.

Kicking an opponent

Kicking one of the other team on purpose is very serious
and players who do it deserve all they get. As well as
watching out for the player who lashes out with his foot in
a moment of temper, and for the homicidal maniac who
launches himself with both feet at an opponent—this could
be interpreted as 'kicking' or 'jumping at an opponent'—
the referee will have an eye open for the calculated 'over
the top' tackle. In this, a player who is apparently going
for the ball in fact lets his foot go over the top of it and
cracks his opponent on the leg. He may then, of course,
protest that it was an accident and be all regrets and
apologies, and the referee must be sure that it was
deliberate before taking action.

Tripping

This is another situation where the referee must decide what the tackler's intention was. It is obvious that in a fair tackle one or both players could fall to the ground in a genuine attempt to play the ball. An example is when the goalkeeper dives at the feet of a forward and secures the ball, over which the forward then falls. The 'keeper was concerned only with getting the ball, and is clearly not at fault if the forward goes down. In this situation, the referee has to be careful not to be taken in by players who, beaten in the tackle, 'take a dive' to make it look as if they have been tripped. Players doing this find themselves in trouble with the ref for 'ungentlemanly conduct' and could be booked for it.

It is not only the legs and feet that can be used for tripping; Law 12 defines the offence as 'throwing or attempting to throw ... by the use of the legs or by stooping in front of or behind' an opponent.

Jumping at an opponent

Jumping at an opponent is a foul. This does not mean that you cannot make bodily contact with an opponent when jumping for a high ball, and it does not mean that sliding tackles cannot be made fairly. The Law is pinpointing the player who launches himself at an opponent with no intention of getting the ball. Law 12 advises referees that 'jumping at an opponent and not jumping for the ball' must be penalised, and that 'There is no such thing as accidental jumping at an opponent'.

Once, in my playing days, we came up against a team whose centre-half (as we used to call them) was so primitive that his own team-mates would go near him only if it was their turn to throw lumps of raw meat into his cage and opponents would tackle him only in threes and fours. In one particular match, they got a free kick about ten yards outside our penalty area, and we lined up a four-man wall, marshalled by Perce from behind. The ref whistled, and out of the gloom (it was November) came this Stone Age remnant, taking a run-up as if he was going to put the ball into orbit. As he got nearer, it became obvious

that that wasn't the idea at all. He ran over the ball and straight at the wall, the intention being to scatter us and make a hole for the bloke behind him to shoot into. He succeeded to the extent that we all got out of his way, but he went on and ran straight into Perce. Perce's customary suavity deserted him, and the ref invited them both to go and take their showers before the rush started. When they came up before the disciplinary committee, Perce said he was sorry for the bad language but he hadn't been able to think of anything worse on the spur of the moment, and the centre-half was suspended for 6 weeks. He retired not long after, but the word in the dressing-room was that his club had put him on the transfer list and that a wildlife park had signed him.

Hand-ball

Handling the ball is defined as carrying, striking or propelling it with the hand or arm, and it must be deliberate to be penalised. It is obviously unfair for a player to be punished when the ball is kicked onto his hand.

Deliberate hand-ball is punished by a direct free kick or a penalty, except in one circumstance. If a defender handles the ball on its way to goal and keeps it out of the goal, that is a direct free kick or penalty, and perhaps a caution or sending-off as well. But if the defender's hand does not stop the ball from entering the goal, the goal stands. So does the booking or the dismissal. You don't get let off because you failed to stop the goal.

The goalkeeper, of course, is allowed to handle the ball within his own penalty area, within the limits laid down by the 'four-step rule'. And the 'keeper is the only player who can throw the ball direct into the opposition's net for a goal. It's a pretty unusual thing to happen, but a long thrower with a strong wind behind him could do it.

The 'advantage rule'

There are occasions during a match when the referee should not stop the action for an infringement, even a serious one, because it would actually be to the advantage of the team committing the offence for a free kick or even a penalty to be awarded, rather than for the game to go on. An attempt at a trip, for instance, might fail and leave the attacker with a clear run on goal, or a defender who handles the ball might actually give it to the other side in a position from which a goal is likely to be scored. In such situations, the offending side would be likely to prefer a free kick, which would give them time to re-group, or a penalty, which could be saved. The referee is instructed, in Law 5, to 'Refrain from penalizing in cases where he is satisfied that, by doing so, he would be giving an advantage to the offending team'. A team must not be allowed to benefit from a foul of its own commission.

The referee has to make an instant judgement about whether a player who has been fouled, or his team, is actually left in an advantageous position which justifies letting play go on. If he decides not to whistle, he cannot later change his mind if the advantage does not come to anything. Once he has let play go on, that's it.

Playing the advantage does not mean that the player who committed the foul cannot be booked or even sent off —the referee can still do this at the next stoppage.

Penalty!

If any of the direct free kick offences is committed inside the penalty area by a member of the defending team, the result is a penalty. It is important, by the way, to realise that the ball itself does not have to be in the penalty area for a penalty kick to be given. An off-the-ball foul in the penalty area is a penalty as long as the ball is in play, even if it is right down the other end. And the award of a penalty does not save the player who gave it away from being booked or sent off if the referee considers that he deserves it.

When a penalty is being taken, everybody except the defending goalkeeper and the taker of the kick must be well out of the way so they cannot immediately interfere with play. This means they must be outside the penalty area and at least ten yards from the ball, which means being outside the penalty arc, too. (The purpose of the arc is to make sure that no one is within ten yards of the ball when it is on the penalty spot.) In addition, everyone must be on the field. This seems at first glance to be a bit unnecessary, but the point is to prevent defenders from crowding the touch-line beside the posts. The 'keeper must be on the goal-line, and must not move his feet until the ball is kicked, and the kick must not be taken until everyone is in position. The ball is in play once it has travelled the distance of its own circumference, and the kicker must not play it again until another player has touched it. Law 14 also states that the ball must be played forward. Those things are obvious enough, but when it comes to offences at penalty kicks, such as encroachment into the area by other players, there are a few complications.

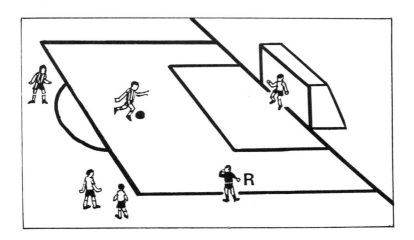

In general, we can say that if the defenders commit an offence, the kick is re-taken unless a goal has been scored anyway. Conversely, if an attacker, other than the kicker himself, infringes, the kick is re-taken only if a goal *is* scored. If it is the kicker who breaks Law 14 when the ball is in play, by for instance playing the ball twice, that's an indirect free kick to the defenders.

Let's look at a few possible situations.

● The referee has signalled for the kick to be taken, and the 'keeper moves his feet before the ball has been kicked. The kick is taken anyway, and if a goal is scored, it stands. If the 'keeper saves, or the shot misses or comes back off the woodwork, the kick has to be re-taken. The same applies, if, having given the signal for the kick to be taken, 'the Referee sees that the goalkeeper is not in his right place on the goal-line'.

● The signal for the kick to be taken has been given, and a defender comes within ten yards or into the area before the ball is in play. The kick is taken, but if no goal is scored, it must be re-taken. What's more, the encroaching player is booked.

● The kicker indulges in what Law 14 calls 'ungentlemanly conduct' during the taking of a kick. If a goal is scored, the kick is re-taken, and the kicker is booked whether or not it is saved.

● The referee has signalled for the kick to be taken but the ball is not yet in play when another attacker enters the penalty area or comes within ten yards. The kick is still taken, but if a goal is scored it has to be taken again. Once more, the trespasser is booked, whatever the result. If the ball rebounds from the 'keeper or from the woodwork, after an attacker has encroached as described, the game is stopped and the defenders are given an indirect free kick from where the attacker intruded.

Things can become even more difficult, however. What happens if the 'keeper moves, and an attacker enters the area, between the giving of the signal and the taking of the kick? Two offences have been committed at the same time by players on opposing sides. Who should be penalised? The answer is simple enough: the kick is re-taken, whether or not a goal is scored, and the invading attacker is booked. The same happens if a defender and an attacker charge in at the same time; the kick is re-taken and they are both booked.

There is also the bizarre possibility of an 'outside agent', perhaps a dog or a spectator, interfering with the ball once it is in play. Law 14 says that if this happens on the ball's way to goal, the kick is re-taken, whether or not a goal is

scored; if it happens when the ball rebounds into play from 'keeper or woodwork, the referee will stop the game and re-start it by dropping the ball at the point where the interference occurred, unless, as explained in 'Dropped ball', it happened inside the goal area, in which case the ball is dropped on the nearest point of the six-yard line parallel to the goal-line.

In normal circumstances, of course, a ball rebounding into play from the taking of a penalty is played in the usual way, except that the kicker is not allowed to touch it again until another player has played it. If it comes back off the 'keeper, then it has been touched by another player and the striker is allowed another shot.

As mentioned in 'Teams and times' (see pages 19–20), time is added on to the end of the first half or at full-time for a penalty to be taken. This raises the point of when a penalty is considered to have been completed. Should the referee allow time for the ball to be put back into the net from a rebound?

The answer to that is no. The penalty is considered to have been completed when the referee has decided whether or not a goal has been scored from the original kick. This means a direct goal counts, and if the ball goes in off the cross-bar, goalposts or 'keeper, that is a goal, too. But once the ball rebounds into play, the referee will whistle and that's the end of it.

Goal!

Law 10, solemnly entitled 'Method of Scoring', states the obvious when it says that 'a goal is scored when the whole of the ball has passed over the goal-line, between the goal-posts and under the cross-bar'. However, it is worth repeating here that the whole of the ball must have crossed the line for a goal to be scored.

The law also specifies that the ball must not be 'thrown, carried, or intentionally propelled by hand or arm' (certain World Cup strikers please note that Law 10 makes no mention of 'the hand of God') 'by a player of the attacking side, except in the case of a goalkeeper, who is within his own penalty area'. There are two points here. First, as we have seen, a goalkeeper can score with a direct throw, and second, if the ball is put into his own net by a defender using his hand or arm, the goal stands (providing the referee has not blown his whistle for the infringement, prior to the ball crossing the goal-line). It would clearly be wrong for a penalty to be given, which might be missed, when the ball is already in the net as the result of a penalty infringement by the defence.

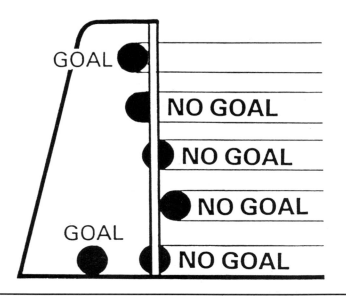

There is also the possibility of an 'outside agent', perhaps a spectator, preventing a goal from being scored or actually 'scoring' one. What happens if this occurs when a penalty is being taken is explained on pages 55–6, but in 'normal' circumstances, the position is as follows.

● Law 10 makes it clear that the referee must not award a goal because the ball was about to enter the net, however obvious it was that that was going to happen. For a goal to be scored, the ball must cross the goal-line. If there is interference, the game must be re-started with a dropped ball at the point where the interference occurred.

● Suppose that a spectator runs on and tries to prevent a goal from being scored. If he fails to touch the ball or does not interfere with play, and the ball goes into the net, that's a goal anyway. If, however, he does make contact with the ball or interferes, perhaps by preventing a defender from reaching the ball and having a chance to clear it, then again there is a dropped ball.

If in either of these two cases the interference occurred within the goal area, the ball is dropped on the nearest point of the six-yard line parallel to the goal-line, which is the usual thing in dropped-ball situations in the six-yard box.

This seems a good moment to repeat that you cannot score direct from a goal kick, a throw-in or an indirect free kick, but you can score from a corner.

Cautions

Law 5 tells referees to 'caution any player guilty of misconduct or ungentlemanly behaviour'; referees have the power to do this from the moment they run on to the field of play.

Misconduct obviously covers bad fouls and 'persistent' infringement of the laws of the game; it also covers such offences as entering the field without the referee's permission once the game has started—this could happen when making a substitution. You can be cautioned for time-wasting (the use of red and yellow cards is permitted only in first team matches in the Football League or F.A. Cup); for dissent about a decision 'by word or action', which includes kicking the ball away at a free kick; for not retiring ten yards at a free kick; and for encroaching into the penalty area when a penalty is being taken (this applies to defenders and attackers, as I mentioned on page 55).

'Ungentlemanly behaviour' covers a multitude of sins: foul play, trips, leaning on the shoulders of one of your own team to gain height in an attempt to head the ball, obstructing or delaying an opponent by stretching your arms and jumping about in front of him even if you don't make bodily contact, and dancing about or gesticulating 'in a way calculated to distract or impede the thrower' at a throw-in (see Law 15). The taker of a penalty may also be guilty of ungentlemanly conduct (Law 14), as well as a goalkeeper who 'intentionally lies on the ball longer than is necessary' (Law 12). So, watch it. The referee will be doing so.

Law 5's 'Advice to Referees' lays down a procedure for the cautioning of a player. The referee must state that the player is being cautioned, and will ask for his name. (It's better to give your real name. Perce once told a ref who was booking him that his name was Groucho Marx. The ref said that he'd guessed that from the funny walk.) The referee must also state that the player will be sent off 'if he persists in misconduct'. He may then enjoy the rest of the game from the comfort of the touchline and can expect to hear from the authorities, to whom the referee will report the matter.

You can, by the way, be booked when on the subs' bench, or when the game is stopped or when the ball is out of play, for instance in a dropped ball situation. However, a free kick or penalty cannot be given for a foul committed before the ball reaches the ground, as it is not actually in play. Officials can also be reported to the authorities, for abuse or for coaching on the touch-line, and so can a trainer who runs on without the referee's permission. Second 'bookable' offences lead to dismissal. Dismissal (or as Law 5 says suspension 'from further participation in the game') will follow a second offence meriting a booking which is committed when a player is about to be cautioned for something else, even though he has not yet been warned. You'd have to be pretty dumb to do this, but it does happen.

Sending off

As well as second bookable offences, there are offences
which get the red card straight away. These are violent
conduct, for example striking an opponent or spitting at
him, serious foul play, and using 'foul or abusive language'.
Again, you don't actually have to be on the field to be 'sent
off' it. Law 12 says quite clearly that any player, 'whether
he is within or outside the field of play', can be guilty of
'ungentlemanly or violent' conduct and of 'foul or abusive
language' and 'shall be dealt with according to the nature
of the offence committed'. Substitutes, too, 'shall be subject
to the authority and jurisdiction of the referee whether
called upon to play or not', as Law 3 (Number Of Players)
puts it.

Referees

Law 5 lists ten responsibilities for referees. A number of them are obvious: the enforcement of the Laws, cautioning, sending off, time-keeping—this includes adding on stoppage time—and noting the score, checking the ball to see that it 'meets with the requirements of Law 2' (see page 14) and signalling for the game to be re-started after stoppages. He must also 'Allow no person other than the players and linesmen to enter the field of play without his permission' (see page 30) and must apply the advantage rule to make sure that in whistling for an offence he does not give an advantage to the offending team (see page 51).

There are two other things that the referee has to do, though many players and spectators might think that what he already has to do is more than enough for any member of a breed so notoriously short-sighted, dim-witted and physically decrepit. Nonetheless, the laws give the ref power to stop the game and even abandon it for a variety of reasons, including weather that makes it impossible for play to continue—such as fog, or rain that waterlogs the

pitch. (The referee is advised to visit the ground well before the match and to refuse to allow it to start if the conditions are too bad.) He may also suspend or abandon a match because of crowd disturbances, and he has discretionary powers to stop play for any other reason if 'he deems such stoppage necessary'.

The referee's remaining duty under Law 5 relates to the treatment of injured players. If a player appears to be seriously injured, the referee is instructed to stop the game and have the player taken off for treatment as soon as possible; but if the injury seems to be only slight, the player has to wait for treatment till the ball goes out of play or there is a stoppage of some sort. Injured players who can get to the touch-line or goal-line are expected to go off and be treated there. Only serious cases are honoured with a visit on the field from the bucket-and-sponge man.

The referee receives useful bits of advice from the F.A. in the rule book (this is not necessarily of the same quality as the advice he can be sure of getting from the terraces). Among other things, the book advises him never to allow the players to crowd round him and put pressure on him to change a decision, and not to try to explain decisions to players or spectators. He is also advised to use signals that indicate what is to happen next, not signals that attempt to justify a decision, and—this will surprise the cynics—to have a thorough knowledge of the Laws, to be completely impartial and to be physically fit and in good training.

The referee is also in charge of the linesmen. Although all linesmen at a high level of competition are qualified referees, it is still the referee's decision that counts. He is not obliged to stop play when a linesman flags, though he may consider his advice and perhaps act on it. He will, of course, stop play when a linesman signals that the ball has gone over the touch-line or goal-line, and if a neutral linesman has something to say about an infringement the referee may not have seen, the referee 'can consider the intervention'. This can even lead to the cancelling of a goal if the linesman has seen something relevant to 'that phase of a game immediately before the scoring of a goal'. However, the referee is told that he must never 'consider the intervention of a Linesman if he himself has seen the incident and from his position on the field, is better able to judge'.

Linesmen

The linesmen, that dedicated and much-maligned body of men, are given three specific jobs to do under Law 6. These are to flag when the ball has gone out of play, to indicate which team is to have the throw-in, goal kick or corner, and to signal to the referee when either side wants to bring on a sub. They are also required to 'assist the Referee to control the game in accordance with the Laws'. This assistance takes the form of pointing out to the referee any foul play or ungentlemanly conduct that they think the ref may not have noticed, and of giving an opinion when the ref asks them for one.

It is perfectly reasonable for the referee to expect this kind of help from neutral linesmen, whom he can use as assistant referees. However, in many minor matches, neutral linesmen are unlikely to be available, and competition rules often require each team to provide a linesman for matches. This is usually the substitute or a club official, for whom it may be difficult to make impartial decisions under pressure. In these circumstances, referees

are advised to use 'club linesmen' in a much more limited way, restricting their responsibilities to signalling when the ball is out of play—the referee may even find it useful to remind them that the ball must be *wholly* over the line— and indicating which team is to put it back in again. We do, of course, see club linesmen flagging for offside, but if the referee has asked them to look out for this, he should also emphasise that his decision is paramount on that and on all other matters, and that they must accept it at once, as players are expected to.

Club linesmen have to do their best to forget their usual loyalties when running the line, difficult though it is. Players can help by not yelling such encouragements to neutrality as 'That's it, Gary, get that flag going, my son!' and 'I told you to watch that number 8, Gary, he's yards offside!'

Conclusion

So there you are—the seventeen Laws of soccer, at its best the world's most thrilling game. And it's at its best when players don't waste time explaining rules they don't actually know to a referee who does know them, and the action flows with the minimum of interruption. It's a game of skill and excitement, not of notebooks and hysteria. As a ref once said to Perce when he'd calmed him down after a misunderstanding with a centre-forward who'd taken a dislike to him, 'Can we get on with the game now?'

Soccer rules—OK?

Index